Here We Grief Again

Surviving a Silenced Heartbeat
(S.A.S.H.) Companion Journal

ANNETTE HARRIS

Here We Grief Again © 2025 by Annette Harris

All Rights Reserved.

Holy Bible, New International Version®, NIV® Copyright ©1973, 1978, 1984, 2011 by Biblica, Inc. Used by permission. All rights reserved worldwide.

Holy Bible, New Living Translation, copyright © 1996, 2004, 2015 by Tyndale House Foundation. Used by permission of Tyndale House Publishers, Inc., Carol Stream, Illinois 60188. All rights reserved.

No part of this book may be reproduced in any form or by any electronic or mechanical means including information storage and retrieval systems, without permission in writing from the author. The only exception is by a reviewer, who may quote short excerpts in a review.

Printed in the United States of America
The Scribe Tribe Publishing Group

TABLE OF CONTENTS

Understand Grief 7

How to Deal With Your New Normal 15

Getting Through the 'Firsts' 25

Get to a Place of Healing 37

Obtain Help 47

How Is Your Grief? 57

References 67

Here We Grief Again! How did we end up here AGAIN? We grieve marriages ending, friendships and relationships disintegrating, homes and places of business being destroyed, financial stability being threatened, dreams and goals running out of steam, mental and physical health deteriorating, and of course death.

The *grief* is coming in stages, waves and tsunamis and consuming our entire beings! I know grief is a part of life, but Lord, can I get a break? I need to be able to come up for air so I can breathe and LIVE!

Did I just describe your experience? Whelp, you are not alone because I have been there!

My first book, *Surviving A Silenced Heartbeat* (S.A.S.H.), addressed the reality of "grief" and how to handle it. I chose to use the word *silenced* and not *silent* in the title because of how each word is defined.

silence *(noun) = the lack of any sound.*

There is a lack of sound that comes from grief and/or grief comes from a lack of sound.

vs.

silent *(adverb) = describes an action.*

You have the ability to speak but you choose not to.

It was not easy to share my personal journey with the world. Because of the grief that I experienced, my own voice was *silenced*!

The good news is I found my voice again, and I want to help you find yours when grief finds its way to you.

In this journal, we'll pick up where *Surviving A Silenced Heartbeat* (S.A.S.H.) ends by encouraging you to:

- understand what grief/loss really is

- be transparent about your own personal journey with grief/loss; this will enable you to pay it forward to help someone else
- seek the help that's needed to 'AWAKEN YOUR SILENCED VOICE' when you end up saying "here we grief" again

Objectives of this Journal:

1. Help you understand GRIEF so that it will not define you or stop you from living

2. Teach you how to deal with your NEW NORMAL

3. Help you get through the 'FIRSTS'

4. Lead you to a place of HEALING

5. Encourage HELP through:

- Counseling
- Resources
- Nutrition
- Purpose
- Love

6. Help you to assess your GRIEF

In January 2023, I created a daily YouTube vlog entitled, *SASH Talk Where Talks Turn To Transformations*, as a safe space for those who needed to understand how and why they are experiencing, handling and dealing with grief! As a certified mental health advocate, I saw this need and decided to use my platform to address it head on.

These same daily one-minute discussions are strategically placed throughout this journal, and they are meant to help anyone to unload their thoughts, release the hurt and let the healing begin!

Although the subjects of discussion are God-inspired and supported by the Word of God, they will address whatever you are dealing with at any given time! *Talks will Turn to Transformations!* You will be motivated to "journal" your way through to transformation!

Remember to be free when journaling. Journaling is healing. Understand that you can't change or control what has already occurred. If you focus on something that's out of your control it works against the progress of healing.

In the midst of dealing with grief remember, it's time for you to speak again!

"God wants to heal you

Everywhere you hurt, everywhere you hurt

God will see you through

He'll take the pain away..."

(lyrics from "God Wants to Heal You"/Ernest Pugh)

HERE WE GRIEF AGAIN!
Composed by: Pastor Kevin McGee

Feeling like I am stuck
In a perpetual cycle
Round and round I go
Dealing with another round of grief
It's becoming second nature to me
Like breathing

As soon as I dry one set of tears
My eyes start raining again
Makes me wonder
If God decided
That I needed to learn
About grief up close and personal
Because if it ain't one thing
It's certainly another

I am experiencing grief so much
That I am forgetting how to grieve
This ring of grief
Has me caged and I don't see an exit

The word says that
We are troubled on every side
Yet not distressed
However, grief
Is not on every side
But it's found its way into me

I need someone to come and help me
Because

Here I go
Here I go again

Grief has become a squatter in my life
And ignores all notices of eviction
It's got me going in circles
Like a whirlpool and I can't break free

And I'm losing my desire to break free
Becoming content with
Being pulled
under and consumed

Dealing with another round of grief

It's becoming second nature to me

Like breathing

UNDERSTAND GRIEF

(SO THAT IT WILL NOT DEFINE YOU OR STOP YOU FROM LIVING)

What is GRIEF?

We all can experience grief daily.

Grief has been defined as the response to the loss of something or someone deemed important. It is a reaction to a significant loss, such as divorce, health, job/career, miscarriage/abortion, mental health challenges, home, financial and death, etc.

What does it affect?

- Your identity (the importance of it)
- Emotion (lack/absence of it)

Stages of GRIEF:

The five stages of grief theory developed by psychiatrist, Elisabeth Kübler-Ross, suggests that we all go through five distinct stages of grief after a major loss: **denial, anger, bargaining, depression, and acceptance.**[1]

- The first stage in this theory, **denial**, helps us minimize the overwhelming pain of loss. As we process the reality of our loss, we are also trying to survive emotional pain. Denial is not only an attempt to pretend that the loss does not exist. We are also trying to absorb and understand what is happening.[2]
- In the second stage, it is common to experience **anger**. We are trying to adjust to a new reality and we are likely experiencing extreme emotional discomfort. There is so much to process that anger may feel like it allows us an

emotional outlet. This can leave you feeling isolated in your experience and perceived as unapproachable by others in moments when we could benefit from comfort, connection, and reassurance.[2]

- When coping with loss in this third stage, it isn't unusual to feel so desperate that you are willing to do almost anything to alleviate or minimize the pain. Losing a loved one or dealing with any kind of loss can cause us to consider any way we can avoid the current pain or the pain we are anticipating. There are many ways we may try to **bargain**.[2]
- During our experience of processing grief in the fourth stage, there comes a time when our imaginations calm down and we slowly start to look at the reality of our present situation. Bargaining no longer feels like an option, and we are faced with what has transpired. Although this is a very natural stage of grief, dealing with **depression** can be extremely isolating.[2]
- When we come to a place of **acceptance**, it is not that we no longer feel the pain of loss. However, we are no longer resisting the reality of our situation, and we are not struggling to make it something different. Sadness and regret can still be present in this phase, but the emotional survival tactics of denial, bargaining, and anger are less likely to be present.[2]

Grief is not linear, which means it does not have a clear beginning and end. I want to make sure that you understand that although the stages of grief are organized from the first to the fifth stage, you may or may not experience all of the stages. There is also the possibility that you will skip stages and/or not go in order from the first stage to the last stage. Don't feel pressured into thinking that you are not dealing with these stages correctly. Remember, every single person will grieve differently. Please do not measure yourself to others or allow people to compare your grief process to theirs or anyone else's.

The most important thing for you to do is take time to heal. It is also crucial for you to seek help from a mental health professional if you find that you are stuck in a certain stage for a long period or if you cannot function as you normally would.

YOUR PAIN HELPS TO TEACH THE WORLD[3]

For the most part, our society is grief-illiterate, but if we share our reality of how we're feeling about grief, it can enlighten and/or educate others.

Remember grief deals with any major loss in your life (death, marriage, financial, career, etc.) and the pain of it can be activated at a moment's notice (song, discussion, activity).

Don't ignore or hide the pain of grief, deal with it straight on. It's ok to allow others to see your vulnerability, it helps you and them deal with the reality of a loss.

Psalm 55v22:
Cast your cares on the Lord and he will sustain you;
he will never let the righteous be shaken.

I Peter 5v7:
Casting all your care upon Him, for He cares for you.

UNDERSTANDING GRIEF COMPONENTS[3]

Grief affects two major components:

1. Your <u>IDENTITY</u> (and the importance of it)

Significant losses will produce holes in:

- your identity
- your behavioral changes
- your self-perception
- your place in the world (it may change)

2. Your <u>EMOTION</u> (or the absence of it)

We get enjoyment from the emotions connected to the person, place or thing that we lost.

To help you maneuver through your loss:

- acknowledge your grief
- seek counseling and therapy
- try to find other things that would generate similar emotions

Psalm 34v18:
The Lord is close to the brokenhearted;
he rescues those whose spirits are crushed

Journal Entry Date _____

My Daily Thoughts

Understanding Grief: How can grief be understood?

_____
_____
_____
_____
_____
_____
_____
_____
_____
_____
_____
_____
_____
_____
_____
_____
_____
_____
_____
_____
_____
_____
_____
_____

Journal Entry Date _____

My Daily Thoughts

Understanding Grief: How can I heal when the feeling of grief is so strong?

_____
_____
_____
_____
_____
_____
_____
_____
_____
_____
_____
_____
_____
_____
_____
_____
_____
_____
_____
_____
_____
_____
_____

HOW TO DEAL WITH YOUR NEW NORMAL

The Collins English Dictionary defines, new normal, as "a hitherto unusual state of affairs that suddenly becomes standard or typical."[12] In other words, things look and feel different after a crisis has occurred. It means that things are not the same because what was considered normal has been replaced.

ACCEPTANCE (STAGE OF GRIEF)

ACCEPTANCE is the fifth and final grief stage of the Kubler-Ross model. While it can solve problems, it's hard to get to this stage.

When you desire something that is out of your control, it does more damage than good. Here are some facts about acceptance found in PsychologyToday.com.[9]

Acceptance:

- doesn't mean you like, want, choose or support what you're accepting. It is an active process and it must be practiced regularly.
- doesn't mean you can't work on changing things.
- doesn't mean it's going to be that way forever.
- can be practiced in all areas of our lives toward (our experience, people, appearance, emotions, ideas, etc.).

Acceptance doesn't mean you're endorsing grief, it just helps you to balance your past and current experiences in your life!

Philippians 4v13:
For I can do everything through Christ, who gives me strength.

I am experiencing grief so much

That I am forgetting how to grieve

This ring of grief

Has me caged and I don't see an exit

FAKE IT TILL YOU MAKE IT!

(www.psychologytoday.com)

"FAKE IT TILL YOU MAKE IT" is an aphorism that suggests that by imitating confidence, competence, and an optimistic mindset, a person can realize those qualities in their real life and achieve the results they seek. But when should we use this aphorism?

In terms of business, financial, industrial, and public trust matters, the adage of "fake it till you make it" is usually disastrous. This corrupted use of the term is mostly based on the tendency for many people to pretend they know something even when they don't.

There is a gigantic difference between "faking" courage when fearful and misrepresenting products, ideas and devices in order to get money from investors.

In behavioral psychology, the idea of "act as if" and "fake it till you make it" can be a pivotal therapeutic intervention. This is simply because it is much easier to act ourselves into feeling better than to think ourselves into feeling better, or be talked into feeling better.

What should we do? First, prove to yourself you can do what you want and that'll convince others that you can do it!

Don't only, "fake it till you make it," make it till you make it!

Romans 12v2:
Don't copy the behavior and customs of this world, but let God transform you into a new person by changing the way you think. Then you will learn to know God's will for you, which is good and pleasing and perfect.

Ephesians 4v22:
Throw off your old sinful nature and your former way of life, which is corrupted by lust and deception.

Philippians 4v8:
And now, dear brothers and sisters, one final thing. Fix your thoughts on what is true, and honorable, and right, and pure, and lovely, and admirable. Think about things that are excellent and worthy of praise.

Journal Entry Date _____

My Daily Thoughts

My New Normal: What will my "my new normal" look and feel like?

_____
_____
_____
_____
_____
_____
_____
_____
_____
_____
_____
_____
_____
_____
_____
_____
_____
_____
_____
_____
_____
_____

Journal Entry Date _____

My Daily Thoughts

My New Normal: How can I focus and adapt to this new state of being?

_____
_____
_____
_____
_____
_____
_____
_____
_____
_____
_____
_____
_____
_____
_____
_____
_____
_____
_____
_____

Here We Grief Again

In a perpetual cycle

Round and round I go

GETTING THROUGH THE 'FIRSTS'

The Most Difficult Time of The Year: Mental Health During the Holidays | NAMI: National Alliance on Mental Illness[8]

The truth is that for many, the holidays can be the most difficult time of the year. In 2014, NAMI found that 64% of people with mental illness said the holidays made their conditions worse. A 2021 survey showed that 3 in 5 Americans felt their mental health was negatively impacted by the holidays.

So, if you find yourself feeling anxious for the holidays, you are certainly not alone. Here are a few steps you can take to prioritize your mental health during this hectic season:

COPING WITH GRIEF DURING THE HOLIDAY AND BIRTHDAY SEASONS[4]

1) Prioritize and plan (make a list of what you would like to accomplish, do or not do during the holiday). For example, plan around traditions, get-togethers, events, decorations, meals or anything that you've done in the past. Sit down with family and allow each person to discuss what they desire to do. Allow everyone a chance to express themselves because everyone will have different emotions. Be creative and leave room for changes or additions to current traditions.
2) Accept your limitations. Grief consumes your energy during any season, but the holidays can add more demands on your time and energy. Lower

your expectations to accommodate your current needs. Be honest with yourself about how you're feeling and know that your needs may change.

3) Accommodate changes that come with your circumstances and find ways to decrease your stress. Consider changing your surroundings or traditions to decrease your stress. Be honest with your family and let them know this year might be different for you. Review and or re-evaluate previously written priorities and leave out unnecessary activities that may overwhelm you.

4) Ask for and accept help. Accept offers of assistance with the holidays, such as with shopping, decorating, cleaning, cooking, etc.

There is NO perfect formula for dealing with grief or loss over the holidays that will make everything better. However, God will help you to deal with your NEW NORMAL.

NO STRESS HOLIDAYS

The Holidays are coming!

This is a time of excitement for some, but for others, maybe not. Does any of the following apply to you:

- Are you getting overwhelmed by the details, either hosting or visiting?
- Are you worried about who to invite or whose invite to accept?
- Are you contemplating what problems will occur at gatherings because of what has transpired in the past?
- Are you comparing your holidays with others on social media?
- Are you experiencing financial stress by spending too much or too little?

If so, try these things:

- Consider how you want your holiday to look and plan it out to fit your own life and obligations.
- Say no to invites that may overwhelm you.
- Host, but don't cook.
- Prepare escape plans just in case controversy erupts.

- Anticipate that others may be stressed as well, so handle them accordingly.
- Remember that doing less is more, but do it in the spirit of excellence.

Romans 12v18:
Do all that you can to live in peace with everyone.
Hebrews 12v14:
Work at living in peace with everyone, and work at living a holy life, for those who are not holy will not see the Lord.
Proverbs 16v9:
We can make our plans, but the Lord determines our steps.
Isaiah 40v30-31:
Even youths will become weak and tired, and young men will fall in exhaustion. But those who trust in the Lord will find new strength. They will soar high on wings like eagles. They will run and not grow weary. They will walk and not faint.

FAMILY TIME DURING THE HOLIDAYS

I see more and more how spending time with family during the holidays, for some, can be difficult. Family relationships can be stressful but knowing how to navigate when spending time with them is a skill!

Triggers that go unaddressed, such as childhood trauma, sexual, physical and mental abuse and disrespected boundaries, can re-emerge during the holidays and this will make for a strained visit. We should consider being a support to family members so they won't feel stressed and alone.

LET'S TRY TO:

1. Be realistic about family ways and plan for any challenges.

2. Set boundaries and say no to things that will negatively affect your mental health.

3. Set your mind to think positively before gathering with your family.

4. Connect with someone who you can vent to, just in case (best friend, other family member).

REMEMBER: We can't choose our blood family, but your response is your power.

Proverbs 22v6:
Direct your children onto the right path,
and when they are older, they will not leave it.
Exodus 20v12:
Honor your father and mother. Then you will live a long,
full life in the land the Lord *your God is giving you.*

MANAGING CHRISTMAS

"Hang all the mistletoe
I'm gonna get to know you better
This Christmas
And as we trim the tree
How much fun it's gonna be together
This Christmas..."
("This Christmas"/Donny Hathaway)

Just like the lyrics of this song, Christmas is a joyous time, but it can be difficult for many.

Many people feel the dread associated with Christmas Day creeping up. They may have lost a loved one, their home, a job, their career, and the list goes on! It can be difficult to acknowledge grief on Christmas. Let's learn how to manage the holiday season for ourselves and others.

- Check on one another.
- Learn to be kind and speak kindly when interacting with each other. You never know what situation they're dealing with or if it is difficult for them to gather with everyone.
- Prioritizing self-care on Christmas Day is essential.

These are important tips to facilitate a very special Christmas for me and you!

James 1v17:
Whatever is good and perfect is a gift coming down to us from God our Father, who created all the lights in the heavens. He never changes or casts a shifting shadow.
John 14v27:
I am leaving you with a gift—peace of mind and heart. And the peace I give is a gift the world cannot give. So don't be troubled or afraid.

CELEBRATING BIRTHDAY(S) OF A DECEASED LOVED ONE

A birthday is the anniversary of the birth of a person. Since we don't only recognize the years lived, it is ok to remember and celebrate them when they're deceased. Some struggle with the anxiety of pain that the birthday can bring on. You may experience sadness because you think about what could have been or what milestone age your loved one did not reach. Everyone is different in how they celebrate. Some ways to celebrate include:

- Creating foundations in a loved one's name or the name of what caused their demise (cancer association, against violence, etc.)
- Connecting with others who are grieving to plan a party or something festive to commemorate them
- Eating special foods that reminds them of their loved one
- Planting trees, flowers, etc.
- Writing letters or birthday cards
- Sharing their feelings on social media

August 14th is my late brother, Darryl's, date of birth. For me, some years are better than others to celebrate, but each year I will continue to honor him through my book, *Surviving a Silenced Heartbeat*!

No matter how you choose to celebrate their birthday, allow yourself to feel and acknowledge your emotions as a way of honoring your loved one. Acknowledge the full range of emotions that remembering them brings out in you, such as sadness, pain, frustration, anger, yearning, appreciation, laughter, warmth, and love.

Journal Entry Date _____

My Daily Thoughts

Getting Through The FIRSTS: How should I plan to celebrate holidays, birthdays, special events after my loss?

_____
_____
_____
_____
_____
_____
_____
_____
_____
_____
_____
_____
_____
_____
_____
_____
_____
_____
_____
_____

Journal Entry Date _____

My Daily Thoughts

Getting Through The FIRSTS: Find a way to celebrate and remember your loss.

_____
_____
_____
_____
_____
_____
_____
_____
_____
_____
_____
_____
_____
_____
_____
_____
_____
_____
_____
_____
_____
_____

I need someone to come and help me

Because

Here I go

GET TO A PLACE OF HEALING

FEEL BROKEN INSIDE? IT'S TIME TO HEAL[3]

Feeling broken inside requires healing, not fixing.

KEY POINTS

- Being human involves pain and struggle.
- Acknowledge that your obstacles aren't going to match up with others and understand that your struggles are essential to healing.
- Do you feel inadequate, unlovable, unworthy? When and how did these feelings begin?
- Find the root cause and the question of why you feel broken. Seek therapy, practice self-awareness, know that you are loved and lovable!

As is noted in the 3rd chapter of Ecclesiastes, there is a time to heal, and you should let that time be NOW!

Ecclesiastes 3v1:
For everything there is a season, a time for every activity under heaven.

WHEN GOD PRAYS FOR YOU

God encourages us to pray, He bids us to come to Him, but what happens when He prays for us?

God will not give up on you like man does because He is faithful to us.

He already knows what is going to happen before we do, what mistakes we may make, and yet He still intercedes...

Luke 22v32
But I have pleaded in prayer for you, Simon, that your faith should not fail. So when you have repented and turned to me again, strengthen your brothers.
Luke 22v40 NLT
"There he told them, "Pray that you will not give in to temptation.""

Remember, when you're going through the pressures of life, God has not given up on you because He prayed for you to be an overcomer!

FINDING PEACE DURING TIMES OF CHAOS

We all seek and typically display some form of control in our lives. When things get out of hand or beyond our control, we may spiral! Some may experience MORE stress than others.

How should we handle this?

First, realize what is and is not under our control and accept it.

Second, let go of control and let God handle it; this will connect you to faith because you have to believe it will work out when you let go.

Try stress reduction techniques such as playing calm music, prayer/meditation, slower pace, deep breaths.

A preventive maintenance tip: Allow God to help you find and nurture your peace now, ahead of any chaotic event!

Philippians 4v7:
Then you will experience God's peace, which exceeds anything we can understand. His peace will guard your hearts and minds as you live in Christ Jesus.

BE HONEST ABOUT HOW YOU'RE DOING

Life can be challenging. And, if someone's mental health is being tested, it can add on extra pressure. The roughest part is feeling like you are alone while going through these struggles.

Many of us are very good at being independent or using our smartphones and not talking to each other. But why would you go through the battles of mental health alone? Why not be honest about how you truly feel instead of saying, "I'm fine" or "I'm okay" when you really are not?

When you recognize and admit to yourself that there is a struggle or challenge occurring then it should force you to take action! Talk to the right people (mentor, therapist, counselor, confidant)!

I always say, "The quickest way to get help is to admit you need it." So please, for your own benefit, be honest about how you're doing!

Psalm 34v17:
The LORD hears his people when they call to him for help.
He rescues them from all their troubles.

SHORTCUTS TO GREATER HAPPINESS

Our feelings derive from our actions and thoughts. Our reality is created in our brain. To assist us in not becoming overwhelmed with what is happening in the world around us, we must change our brain's thinking:

- be grateful
- embrace challenges
- do something we love
- help someone else
- sleep, eat healthy, and exercise
- be kind to ourselves
- speak positively

- develop our relationship with God

What are your shortcuts or tips to greater happiness?

> ***Philippians 4v11:***
> ***Not that I was ever in need,***
> ***for I have learned how to be content with whatever I have.***
> ***Psalm 119v47:***
> ***How I delight in your commands! How I love them!***

HEALED PEOPLE HEAR DIFFERENTLY!

Healing is powerful! When it is fully experienced, our view of the world changes and our emotional state will greatly benefit. Despite trauma and setbacks, healed people learn to listen clearly! But if we continue to carry the unresolved hurt, there is no way to tune in! If we are hurt, we will typically stand up and defend ourselves.

You're not alone in whatever it is you are dealing with. Find your support system and seek wisdom to move forward.

LISTEN to the strength that's within you.

LISTEN to how to build your future (it may be different from what you originally thought).

LISTEN to your past mistakes so that you can break free from any mental bondage.

LISTEN and reconnect with your body.

LISTEN to stop reliving the trauma.

LISTEN without judgment and RESPOND without hurt.

Matthew 13v15:

*For the hearts of these people are hardened,
and their ears cannot hear, and they have closed their eyes—so their eyes cannot see, and their ears
cannot hear, and their hearts cannot understand,
and they cannot turn to me and let me heal them*

Journal Entry Date _____

My Daily Thoughts

Place of Healing: Can I truly experience COMPLETE healing?

_____
_____
_____
_____
_____
_____
_____
_____
_____
_____
_____
_____
_____
_____
_____
_____
_____
_____
_____
_____
_____
_____
_____
_____
_____

Journal Entry Date _____

My Daily Thoughts

Place of Healing: Take time, practice & receive love to heal.

_____
_____
_____
_____
_____
_____
_____
_____
_____
_____
_____
_____
_____
_____
_____
_____
_____
_____
_____
_____
_____

OBTAIN HELP

If grief is a normal and natural reaction to loss, you may wonder why it is so hard to deal with. Maybe it is you or someone you love that needs help getting through this difficult time. Unresolved grief is not easy to deal with, but it needs to be addressed in order to eliminate and/or maneuver through those feelings of pain and sadness connected to your loss. Be encouraged because help is available through professional counseling services, resources, nutrition, purpose and love.

COUNSELING

Mental health professionals work in various capacities to diagnose, treat, and offer medical and physical care to individuals suffering from mental illnesses and disorders.[6] They include:

- Psychologists
- Psychiatrists
- Counselors

RESOURCES

Finding a way to integrate that loss into your life may be a slow process. In order to get to the place of a sense of peace and possibly acceptance, please check out nationwide resources available to you. If you or someone you know needs help, dial 988 or call 1-800-273-8255 for the National Suicide Prevention Lifeline. You can also get support via text by visiting suicidepreventionlifeline.org/chat. Outside of the U.S., please visit the International Association for Suicide Prevention for a database of resources.[7]

MENTAL HEALTH RESOURCES[5]

Too often, people with mental illness do not receive a mental health response when experiencing a mental health crisis. Instead, people in crisis often encounter law enforcement and crowded emergency departments rather than a mental health professional. People in crisis deserve better.

In 2020, the nation took a significant step forward with the enactment of the National Suicide Hotline Designation Act, and NAMI (National Alliance on Mental Illness) advocated a bill that created a nationwide three-digit number (988) to assist people experiencing a mental health or suicidal crisis. The Federal Communications Commission (FCC) determined that this number would be available by phone and text as of July 2022, and is now available across the country. Compassionate, accessible care and support is available for anyone experiencing mental health-related distress.

I John 4v18:
Such love has no fear, because perfect love expels all fear.
If we are afraid, it is for fear of punishment, and this shows
that we have not fully experienced his perfect love.
2 Timothy 1v7:
For God has not given us a spirit of fear and timidity,
but of power, love, and self-discipline.
Isaiah 41v10:
Don't be afraid, for I am with you. Don't be discouraged,
for I am your God. I will strengthen you and help you.
I will hold you up with my victorious right hand.

NUTRITION

SIT DOWN AND EAT

Psalm 23v5
You prepare a feast for me in the presence of my enemies. You honor me by anointing my head with oil. My cup overflows with blessings.

"Are you hungry? Sit down and eat!"

Our natural parents made sure to feed us, under any circumstance. No or low money, no or low food, when it was raining and storming out, when they were fired or couldn't find a job. Sometimes they went without to make sure we had enough. So, it is with God! He sees your adversaries, but He understands that you still need to eat!

Don't allow your appetite to be spoiled by what anyone says or does to you.

SIT DOWN AND EAT!

PURPOSE

CAN YOU FIND YOUR STRONG?

Romans 15v1:
We who are strong must be considerate of those who are sensitive about things like this. We must not just please ourselves.

That sounds like a tall order to fill but I'm sure you'd rather be the one who can help instead of one who needs help. You're going to need strength to do that! Can you "find your strong?"

This means finding the will to keep going when you feel like giving up, managing stress, finding balance and building resilience. You will experience confidence and resilience for yourself and others. One expert created a model to "find their strong" by:

- Getting out of the weeds: being overly busy to the point of losing productivity and meaning (create habitual schedules and systems).
- Knowing your sentence: This is a simple way to identify what your purpose is.
- Building meaningful connections with others. Good relationships are a must.
- Finding your smile. Fight back with humor.[10]

Let's find our STRONG so that we can help others and not just ourselves!

LOVE

PASS THE COMFORT!

We can ease or alleviate a person's feeling of grief or distress by giving a few words of comfort or consoling an individual who is broken.

Let's help each other to deal with these feelings of discomfort, distress and suffering. When you distribute or pass the comfort, you:

- help them to maintain functionality
- help them to develop effective communication
- help them to feel a sense of safety and security
- help to enhance family and meaningful relationships
- help them experience relief of physical symptoms
- help them to benefit from positive psychological and spiritual health

2 Corinthians 1v4
"He comforts us in all our troubles so that we can comfort others. When they are troubled, we will be able to give them the same comfort God has given us."

This scripture is the reason why we should care enough to PASS THE COMFORT!

DO YOU LOVE YOURSELF?

Galatians 5v14:
"For the whole law can be summed up in this one command: "Love your neighbor as yourself."

Galatians, chapter 5 talks about freedom in Christ and one way to experience it is by loving others as yourself.

Although this scripture is a command, I ask…but do you love yourself?

Do you know how you would like to be treated? Once you figure that out then you can genuinely express your love for others.

> ### *Galatians 5v15:*
> *"But if you are always biting and devouring one another, watch out! Beware of destroying one another."*

When we always serve ourselves, we'll always be in conflict with others!

Fall in love with taking care of yourself.

Talk to yourself like someone you love.

LOOKING FOR LOVE?

This may sound foreign to some and familiar to others but God loves you!

HOW?

With unfailing and everlasting LOVE

> ### *Jeremiah 31v3:*
> *Long ago the Lord said to Israel: "I have loved you, my people, with an everlasting love. With unfailing love I have drawn you to myself.*

WHEN?

All the time! He loved us while we were still sinners.

> ### *Romans 5v8:*
> *But God showed his great love for us by sending Christ to die for us while we were still sinners.*

No matter who we are or what we've done!

WHY?

He isn't just loving, but He is the very definition of love.

He loves us because He created us. His affection is unconditional.

He both generates and demonstrates love — and that love endures forever. (Psalm 100:5)

He created you.

Christ died for you.

He is jealous over you.

He wants a relationship with you

GOD LOVES YOU EVEN WHEN YOU DONT LOVE YOURSELF!

Journal Entry Date _____

My Daily Thoughts

Obtaining Help: Reach deep within to find your help.

_____
_____
_____
_____
_____
_____
_____
_____
_____
_____
_____
_____
_____
_____
_____
_____
_____
_____
_____
_____
_____
_____

Here We Grief Again

Journal Entry Date _____

My Daily Thoughts

Obtaining Help: We help others by getting help ourselves.

_____
_____
_____
_____
_____
_____
_____
_____
_____
_____
_____
_____
_____
_____
_____
_____
_____
_____
_____
_____

Here We Grief Again

HOW IS YOUR GRIEF?

I was talking to an individual once who was grieving a family separation and I asked them how they were doing. Their response, "I do not know how to respond anymore," stuck with me!

ARE YOU A "WELL" BEING?

What does this look like for you: happy, content, satisfied, in control, productive? What needs to occur for these things to happen? Are you motivated to be well? Or do you procrastinate completing tasks that will cultivate your wellness only because it makes you uncomfortable?

One statement that I saw in this article is true, "In order to become a 'well' being, we must acknowledge and work with the parts of ourselves that tend to limit our progression." Self-awareness is key in maintaining your health and authentic connections. Don't engage in self-sabotage, but move toward a state of greater self-acceptance, resilience, and overall peace.[11]

What are your non-negotiables of things that nourish and support you? Once we understand what holds us back and address it, then we can focus on our own personal growth and become a well being.

Jeremiah 30v17:
I will give you back your health and heal your wounds," says the Lord.
"For you are called an outcast— 'Jerusalem for whom no one cares.'"
3 John 1v2:
Dear friend, I hope all is well with you and that you
are as healthy in body as you are strong in spirit.

RELIEVE THE PRESSURE

"Relieve the pressure" is equal to the use of persuasion, influence, taking action to improve a situation or using intimidation to make someone do something!

Pressures include but are not limited to, living up to others' standards, self-criticism (comparing self to others), not measuring up, or pushing yourself to the edge. Inside or outside pressures will activate dopamine levels. When goals are not fulfilled, dopamine levels plunge and bring pressure.

To relieve the pressure:

- Listen to your body and your heart.
- Be easier on yourself.
- Slow things down.
- Figure out what's a priority and give yourself the gift of time.
- Be aware of blaming yourself for the things you 'should have' done.

Lift up your hands to relieve the pressure as in ***Psalm 134v2: Lift your hands toward the sanctuary, and praise the LORD.***

HOW IS YOUR GRIEF?

Instead of asking someone how they're doing when they're obviously grieving, maybe you can ask them about their grief?

During horrible times of racial injustice, civil unrest, unemployment, low educational achievement, loneliness, mental health challenges, suicide, devastating weather systems, etc., many are experiencing grief on a different level. Grief is in the heart of everything. People tend to anticipate bad things to occur. There's a lot of ambiguity and uncertainty going on and it creates anticipatory grief. Being vague or receiving information that is defined as vague is not an ideal situation to be in. You wonder what's going to happen before, during and after.

One thing is for sure, there's going to be a need for therapy in the aftermath of said trauma.

One doctor suggested that resiliency and "adaptive capacity" may be a way to help individuals to cope prior to any trauma.

You that are literally in the thick of things or you're concerned about your loved ones that are! Please know that I am praying with you to overcome your grief! When you come out of the "storm" you won't be the same person who walked in.

John 16v22:
So you have sorrow now, but I will see you again; then you will rejoice, and no one can rob you of that joy.

.

DO'S AND DONT'S OF GRIEF SAYINGS

Are you that person who wants to help the grieving, but you don't know what to say or do?

Since experiencing a major loss (death, miscarriage, job, home, divorce, etc.) looks different for everyone, there is no cookie-cutter template to follow but here are some things to keep in mind:

- Allow the grieving person to know that they should own their feelings as long as they need to. There is no timetable they must follow.
- Allow your previous knowledge of that individual to guide your responses. For example, a simple question of "how are you" may offend that person when they are grieving.
- To avoid minimizing the major loss, stay away from phrases such as "everything happens for a reason" or *at least'* statements: "at least' they didn't suffer" or "at least you can try to have children again."
- If you don't know what to say, be honest with the grieving individual(s) and they will appreciate your willingness to help.

Be consistent and be there for them as often and as long as you can; sometimes you may just need to sit in silence and let them vent.

Matthew 5v4:
God blesses those who mourn, for they will be comforted.

If you or someone you know needs counseling or therapy, please visit

Psychology Today to find a therapist.

Journal Entry Date _____

My Daily Thoughts

How is your grief? What stage are you in?

_____
_____
_____
_____
_____
_____
_____
_____
_____
_____
_____
_____
_____
_____
_____
_____
_____
_____
_____
_____

Journal Entry Date _____

My Daily Thoughts

How is your grief? Be honest about where you are in the process.

_____
_____
_____
_____
_____
_____
_____
_____
_____
_____
_____
_____
_____
_____
_____
_____
_____
_____
_____
_____
_____
_____
_____
_____

Here We Grief Again

REFERENCES

[1] Elisabeth Kübler-Ross PMC www.nih.gov

[2] www.verywellmind.com

[3] Feel Broken Inside? It's Time to Heal | Psychology Today

[4] www.griefshare.org

[5] www.nami.org

[6] www.indeed.com

[7] www.msn.com

[8] The Most Difficult Time of The Year: Mental Health During the Holidays | NAMI: National Alliance on Mental Illness

[9] www.psychologytoday.com

[10] Find Your Strong: 8 Ways to Perform at Your Best | Psychology Today

[11] Are You a "Well" Being? | Psychology Today

[12] https://www.collinsdictionary.com/dictionary/english/the-new-normal

scan to
check-in on your Mental Wellness

SCAN ME

SCAN ME

SCAN ME

SCAN ME

Scan the QR code to be on the road to promoting and receiving mental wellness!